Kid Pick!

Title: _____

Author: _____

Picked by: _____

_____

Why I love this book:

_____

_____

_____

Children's Catalog

Sports and My Body

Swimming

Charlotte Guillain

Heinemann Library
Chicago, Illinois

www.heinemannraintree.com
Visit our website to find out
more information about
Heinemann-Raintree books.

To order:

☎ Phone 888-454-2279

🖥 Visit www.heinemannraintree.com
to browse our catalog and order online.

© 2009 Raintree
an imprint of Capstone Global Library, LLC
Chicago, Illinois

Customer Service: 888-454-2279

Visit our website at www.heinemannraintree.com

Edited by Siân Smith, Rebecca Rissman, and
Charlotte Guillain
Designed by Joanna Hinton-Malivoire
Picture research by Ruth Blair
Production by Duncan Gilbert

Originated by Chroma Graphics (Overseas) Pte. Ltd
Printed and bound in China by South China Printing
Company Ltd

13 12 11 10 09
10 9 8 7 6 5 4 3 2 1

Library of Congress Cataloging-in-Publication
Guillain, Charlotte.
  Swimming / Charlotte Guillain.
    p. cm. -- (Sports and my body)
  Includes bibliographical references and index.
  ISBN 978-1-4329-3455-2 (hc) -- ISBN 978-1-4329-
3460-6 (pb) 1. Swimming--Juvenile literature. I. Title.
  GV837.6.G85 2008
  797.2'1--dc22
                              2009007083

Acknowledgments
The author and publishers are grateful to the following
for permission to reproduce copyright material:
Alamy pp. **10** (© Martin Strmiska), **19**, **23** (© Richard
Levine); Corbis pp. **4** (Reix—Liewig/For Picture), **6**
(Jan Butchofsky-Houser), **12** (Annie Griffiths Belt),
15 (Scott McDermott), **23** (Annie Griffiths Belt), **23**
(Scott McDermott), **23** (Reix—Liewig/For Picture);
Gett Images pp. **11** (Leander Baerenz/Photonica), **13**
(David Madison), **16** (Tracy Frankel), **20** (ColorBlind
Images); iStockphoto **22**, **22** (© Martin Pernter), **22**
(© Rafa Irusta); Photolibrary pp. **8** (Purestock), **14**
(Flirt Collection), **17**, **18** (Radius Images), **21** (Burke/
Triolo Productions); Science Photo Library pp. **7**, **23**
(Bill Bachmann); Shutterstock pp. **5** (© Gert Johannes
Jacobus Vrey), **9** (© Sander Rom).

Cover photograph of swimmer reproduced with
permission of Getty Images/China Photos. Back
cover photographs reproduced with permission of
iStockphoto: 1. child in swimming cap; 2. swimming
goggles (© Martin Pernter).

Every effort has been made to contact copyright holders
of material reproduced in this book. Any omissions will
be rectified in subsequent printings if notice is given to
the publishers.

Disclaimer
All the Internet addresses (URLs) given in this book were
valid at the time of going to press. However, due to the
dynamic nature of the Internet, some addresses may
have changed, or sites may have changed or ceased to
exist since publication. While the author and publishers
regret any inconvenience this may cause readers, no
responsibility for any such changes can be accepted by
either the author or the publishers.

Contents

What Is Swimming? 4

How Do I Learn to Swim? 6

How Do I Use My Arms? 8

How Do I Use My Legs? 10

How Do I Use the Rest of My Body? . . 12

What Happens to My Body
    When I Swim? 14

How Does It Feel to Swim? 16

How Do I Stay Safe Swimming? 18

Does Swimming Make Me Healthy? . . 20

Swimming Equipment 22

Glossary 23

Index 24

Find Out More 24

Some words are shown in bold, **like this**. You can find them in the glossary on page 23.

What Is Swimming?

Swimming is exercise we do in water. You can swim in the ocean or in a swimming pool.

Some people swim in competitions and races. Other people just swim to keep fit and have fun.

How Do I Learn to Swim?

You need an adult to teach you how to swim. A teacher from your school or a swimming teacher could teach you at a swimming pool.

To start you need to get used to putting your face in the water. You might use **floats** to help you learn to swim.

How Do I Use My Arms?

You use your arms to pull yourself through the water. You can move your arms in different ways, called **strokes**.

You can use your arms to push down on the side of the pool so you can climb out.

How Do I Use My Legs?

You use your legs to kick. This helps you to move through the water. When you kick hard, you swim faster.

You use your legs when you jump or dive into the pool. You should bend your knees before you jump.

How Do I Use the Rest of My Body?

You can **float** on your back near the top of the water.

You can learn how to hold your breath and open your eyes underwater. You can move your head up or to the side to breathe when you swim.

What Happens to My Body When I Swim?

When you get into the pool the water might make you feel colder. As you swim you will feel warmer and you will breathe faster.

muscle

Your heart will start to beat faster. The **muscles** in your arms and legs will feel tired.

How Does It Feel to Swim?

Swimming is a good way to have fun. You might make new friends as you swim together.

It feels good to get better at swimming. When you swim farther or faster you might get a special trophy or medal.

How Do I Stay Safe Swimming?

Always listen to your teacher or the **lifeguard**. Make sure you know the rules at the swimming pool.

Never run by the pool because you could slip. Before you jump into the pool, check that nobody is in the way and that the water is deep enough.

Does Swimming Make Me Healthy?

Swimming is good exercise and will help to keep you fit. To stay healthy you also need to get plenty of rest.

You should also eat healthy food
every day and drink plenty of water.

Swimming Equipment

goggles

swim cap

towel

Glossary

 **float** stay near the top of water

 **floats** things that float in water and can be used to help people learn to swim

 **lifeguard** someone who works at a swimming pool or on a beach, who helps people to stay safe in the water

 **muscle** part of your body that helps you to move. Exercise can make muscles bigger and stronger.

 **stroke** in swimming a stroke is a movement you make with your arms or legs to help you move through the water

Index

breathe 13, 14

equipment 22

exercise 4, 20, 23

fit 5, 20

float 7, 12, 23

heart 15

jump 11, 19

kick 10

learn 6, 7, 13

lifeguard 18, 23

muscle 15, 23

rules 18, 19

safety 18, 19

stroke 8, 23

Find Out More

http://kidshealth.org/kid/watch/out/water.html
Find out how to stay safe in and around water.

www.usaswimming.org
This Website has information about how to get involved with swimming.